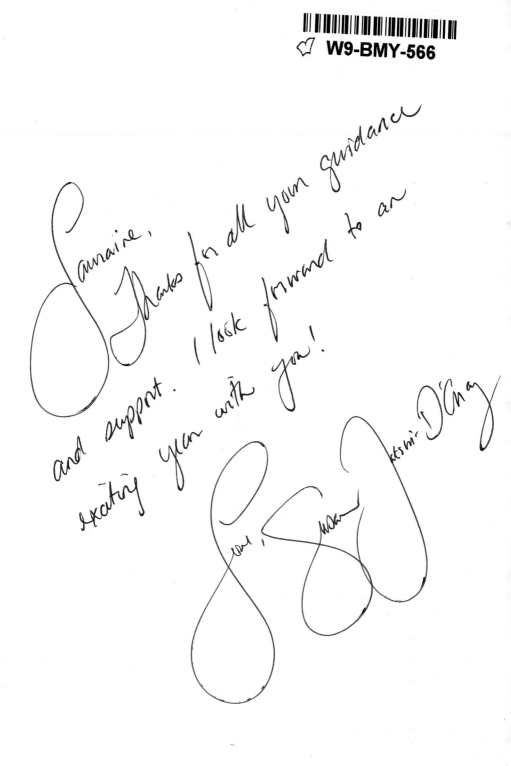

Lorraine,

Thanks for all your guidance and support. I look forward to an exciting year with you!

Love, Susan Jasmin O'Chay

Table of Contents

INTRO   5

CHAPTER 1   25

ProjectMERIT

CHAPTER II   30

Why do a Project?

CHAPTER III   33

Getting Started

CHAPTER IV   46

Research: Is Your Idea Viable?

CONCLUSION   97

INTRO

If you are like most college-bound students, you have heard nightmare stories about friends or acquaintances with 4.0 GPAs or higher and near-perfect SAT scores being rejected from top universities like Harvard and Stanford. While this may be true in isolated circumstances, it is not at all the norm. The reason you hear these horror stories is because it makes a good story for the media.

No need to panic! Only a small percentage of all colleges in the United States and the world are so exclusive that they only select the top tier of all applicants. An encouraging 63.3 % of high school graduates were enrolled in colleges or universities in October of 2011, according to the U.S. Bureau of Labor Statistics. There are countless ways to get the education that suits your individual needs, and many options you haven't even heard of yet, so keep reading to find out how ProjectMerit will improve your chances of getting into the college of your dreams.

Three Ingredients for College Admittance

In the 33 years I have been working as an educational consultant, I have found the most effective formula for college admittance consists of three ingredients:

1) Good grades

2) Good test scores

3) Completion of an individual project (ProjectMerit)

Some of you may be saying, "I've already finished projects- science projects, art projects- my senior year journal. Been there- done that."

Doesn't it seem like everyone has an opinion on what you should do to get into college? Do you ever wonder if their advice is one-size-fits all? I'm here to tell you, it's not. But because of the fact that you are reading this book, I know you have enough drive to go the extra mile for success.

What is the difference between ProjectMerit and any other project?

The term "project" is a broad one. The kind of project I suggest you use your time for is not an internship at the local hospital or joining the leadership club or the tennis team (although these projects may be very worthwhile for you). The beginning of high school is a time when you may be very used to signing up for whatever the "grown ups" are telling you to sign up for. Often times it is those same grown ups who are enlisting you for these activities, because, they say, it will get you into college. Let's just say that you are very accustomed, at this point in your schooling, to do what is expected of you. You are a high-achiever, and you want to go to a good college. What if I were to tell you that doing a project from a great idea that came from you (not from a teacher or parent) would put you on the top of the list at your dream college? You would do it, right? I'm here to tell you, this is not your typical route. Most kids do what is expected of them and nothing more, at least, unless they are forced to. Colleges are as competitive as ever these days, and ProjectMerit gives you just the edge you need to stand out.

An individual project, or ProjectMerit, is something of your own creation. It is your personal vision and your "deep down in your guts" hope for this world. It is making your mark in the world out of something you believe in. As you plan your project, your blood will be pumping with adrenaline because your heart is also invested in it. It is important that you get to know yourself so that you can flesh out something that means something to you. You are going to have to reach deep inside to find out what gets you moving. You will be on and off the computer, making phone calls, meeting with others in the community, reading interesting books and learning, first-hand, how the big world out there works.

Believe in something... and act on that belief

The good news is: College admissions love to admit students who believe in something and have acted on that belief. College admissions are selective, and they don't want you to be just like everyone else. They want you to have good ideas and the drive and ambition to follow through on these ideas. This individual project will bring your college application to the next level and set you apart from the rest. It is time to really consider the four-year formula that will help you beat the college admissions game.

Now we must begin at just the right point. Timing is important. Before you choose a college and start the application process, you first need to consider what careers interest you. This does not have to be a final decision or the end-all-be-all, yet you should know which subjects pique your interest, and also, nonetheless importantly, what you have an aptitude for.

If you picture your future self starting a boutique clothing shop downtown, but you have your mind set on impressing your dad by going to the same law school he did, you will both be disappointed when you get out in the world and have no use for an expensive law degree because you dislike the business of law, and you end up quitting the profession. You would be better served at a top-notch business and fashion program, learning the skills and making the connections you need to open up that boutique you always wanted.

Make sure you have an interest in the subject you pursue.

The world is a better place when people follow their true calling. You probably don't like it when people lie to you. It is just as important for you to tell the truth about yourself. In other words: there is only one you. There is already one of your dad. Your dad isn't going to be the one living your life- going to law classes, studying to pass the bar exam, working as a lawyer five or six days a week. You will be living this life, so find out what your interests are so that you don't waste too much time following a career that is designed for someone else.

Once you know the general subject you are drawn to- be it business, Spanish, music, computer science, psychology or engineering, you can now find the college that has the best program in your field. Schools vary widely in the types of degrees they offer, so you need to find a college that offers a degree in your field of interest. If your dream is to become a nurse, it would make no sense to apply to Harvard because

Harvard does not offer a nursing program. You are a great student. You want to succeed (and Yale is among the best of universities). As big-name colleges are the craze, (and it is really fun to tell everyone you are going to an Ivy League School) you still need to ask: Will this university provide the best education for my field of interest and prepare me for a career I will enjoy?

One big misconception about good colleges is that they offer every major. Private colleges often have specialties just like the shops in your town. You wouldn't go to the best yogurt shop in town expecting to find a hamburger, just as you wouldn't apply to a business school like University of Pennsylvania Wharton expecting to find a psychology program. If your whole family graduated Cal Berkeley, and you want to go there just for the sweatshirt and the bumper sticker, you need to step back and examine what you want out of a college. Does it offer a major in the field you wish to pursue? Is the program a good one? After you delve a little deeper, you may be surprised to find that the selective college you had your heart set on since you were 10-years-old isn't the best choice for you.

Do your homework

The term, "Do your homework," has never been so important in your life. Do the homework to find out if your dream college offers a good program in your major. If you do, the reward is a positive college experience.

Typically, student's parents ask for my college advisory services as soon as their child enters high school, the same age I advise kids to begin the idea incubation of ProjectMerit, but when I first met with Donna*, she was in her junior year of high school, and had already accepted admittance to UC Santa Barbara.

Donna's Story

Donna* had not completed a college worksheet or career test, but she clearly knew her interests were in the marketing realm, and she spent many hours happily working at her parent's Chinese restaurant. She told me she pictured herself owning and managing her own restaurant one day. Donna and her parents hadn't spent the time researching which colleges offered marketing majors, and made the assumption that UC Santa Barbara had everything she would need, simply because the school was of the University of California system, and considered to be a top college. The big problem was: UC Santa Barbara did not offer a marketing program. California state universities and other unique private colleges had much better applied marketing programs and would have been a much better fit for Donna.

Donna and her parents had already committed to UCSB and did not want to budge on the matter. I helped Donna choose an economics major (the closest we could get to a marketing major) and hoped for the best.

Because she entered college on a lackluster path, Donna's first year was rough. She found the economics classes to be ultimately boring and disconnected from the hands-on learning she preferred and excelled in. After floundering for many months, Donna dropped out of college completely.

Donna, like so many other young people, had missed the first step of the college admissions game. She assumed a good college had everything she, as an individual, needed. Every person has a unique path and chart of interests and passions wired into their self. She did fine in high school, when every student had their share of boredom before they graduated, yet college is different. This is the place to really focus on the area of work that you like. In college, you hand pick every class you take. You have a certain amount of credits you need to achieve to earn a degree in your major, but these should all be classes that you have interest in because you chose this route. In high school everyone needs to take English, geometry and civics. In college, if you are in a journalism program, you may have a semester that consists of classes like: Magazine Writing, Law of Communication, Modern Literature, Oceanography and Linguistics. The Oceanography and Linguistics may not be directly related to journalism, but in your first couple of years you will be choosing some classes to fulfill some general requirements in math, science and English.

Pinpointing your interests and gathering information on colleges takes some initiative on your part. Though it may seem like a daunting task, you do not have to do all this research by yourself. Seek the guidance of someone who can help, such as a parent or academic counselor.

Maybe you have many interests and find it hard to choose just one. Maybe you change your mind often. One day you can envision yourself as a doctor. Another day you can see yourself designing computer programs. Even if you had already told your parents you were going to go to medical school, if you have other interests besides medicine, now is the time to explore the options. High school is the perfect time to try internships in professions that interest you. Internships are great ways to peek into a profession to see if you like it.

You can also explore your career options by taking career tests and personal assessments. The sooner you find out what kind of work you like to do, the sooner you can set your mind on a college.

Once you have your career interests narrowed down, you can make intelligent choices about which colleges you should apply to. Most colleges have information online and at the career center at school. When you find the college that has the major you are interested in, the big questions you are going to need to ask are: Will I feel comfortable at this college? Does the community feel like home to you? It is best to visit prospective college campuses and sign up for a guided tour to see for yourself if it is the right fit. Colleges are located in big cities and small towns, and have thousands of students or hundreds of students. Which environment suits your needs?

Now that you found your dream college...

Let's say you spent your time researching colleges and you have found the one (or two) that offers a major in your field of interest. Congratulations. You are ready for what can seal the deal when it comes to getting admitted to your dream college. You are ready to begin ProjectMerit. I have counseled many young students through this process, but with this book as your guide, I think you can do this on your own,.

Bella's Story

Bella* is one of ProjectMerit's best success stories. She was in her second year of high school when her parents signed her up for my college advisory. Though she was an academic high-achiever, I noticed she rarely got excited about much. She led a privileged life by most economical standards, but didn't feel like she "fit- in." Bella felt disconnected from what was going on in the world and had little input when it came to social issues. In her favor, Bella was naturally bright and had a certain charisma that would catch the interest of people she met. Her G.P.A. was good and she was one of the school's top girls' basketball players.

Bella hadn't a clue what she wanted to be "when she grew up," yet she did know one thing for sure: Her college of choice was Santa Clara University. It was a college near her hometown. It had a great reputation and a beautiful campus. As I do with all my new clients, we began the project college advisory process by discussing Bella's take on the world. We talked about politics and environmental issues. She took personality tests and career assessment quizzes. We tried thinking up products that needed to be invented, non-profits that could be started, and new laws that should be written. Yet nothing seemed to get Bella's heart pumping fast. Nothing we talked about would make Bella sit up tall in her chair. This process went on for months (to the dismay of her father, who had to pay me by the hour). I didn't want to choose the subject of her project for her, and I felt the pressure of time hanging over my head. ProjectMerit must be from your own heart and soul, and so I wondered when she would finally find that something she really cared about.

Then one day she came in to my office holding a bottled water.

"Did you know there are traces of antibiotics and hormones in our public water?" I asked, thinking this might be another time when she just shrugged off my attempts to stoke her fire. My husband works in the environmental field, and I had heard his complaints about the water treatment plants in our area. "They don't have the money to pay for the machinery that purifies the left-over pills that people take and flush or pee down the toilet into the water system. They only treat bacteria that causes E. coli and other diseases," I said, "We are drinking, bathing and using all sorts of antibiotics and drugs. Blood pressure meds. Anti-depressants. Steroids. A whole cocktail of pharmaceuticals."

She didn't believe me, so I picked up the phone and dialed the local wastewater treatment facility.

"Does your treatment plant test for pharmaceutical drugs?" I asked. To involve Bella in the conversation, I put the man on speaker phone. She was slouching in her chair, idly sipping her bottled water. The man on the line said, "No we don't." I looked at Bella. Her eyebrows were raised. I asked why. He replied, "That costs too much. We can't fund that kind of testing and we don't have money for the machines that can purify the water of pharmaceuticals."

"We are drinking drugs?" Bella asked. I nodded.

"This is so corrupt!" Bella said. She had gotten up from her chair. "That's nuts! They can't do that!"

And then Bella's project was born. Over the next two years, Bella had taken on the role as a health advocate and worked on passing a new legislation to protect the purity of our drinking water. The more she educated herself on the drugs in our water systems, the more motivated she became to promote change. She set up an outreach program to teach consumers not to flush their expired or unused medications down the toilet. She worked on ways to divert the drugs from our water systems in safe containers that she designed herself and had engineers make. Realizing the economic and political resistance from some of the big pharmacies and drug companies, she approached a United States Senator and won his "It Ought to Be a Law" contest by drafting a proposal that required drug stores to take environmental responsibility of disposing of the public's unused pharmaceuticals.

Two years into her project, Bella was applying to colleges (15 to be exact). Her average G.P.A. was a 3.2 and her test scores were very low. She did not test well at all, something that is common among many of my brightest clients. In her favor was the college essay portion of the application. She had written passionately about her pharmaceutical disposal project. The essay was nothing short of fantastic.

Because of her dynamic essay, she received acceptance letters from 13 of the 15 colleges she applied to, which was a big accomplishment, only Bella's reaction was sheer disappointment. Her top two choices- University of Santa Clara and University of Portland- had denied her admittance.

But Bella was persistent and while immersed in ProjectMerit, had learned a great deal about tenacity. The pharmaceutical disposal legislation she had created and lobbied for had just become a law. The media was all over the story and Bella's face was, literally, on every news channel. She e-mailed both University of Santa Clara and the University of Portland and informed them that the proposed legislation she wrote about in her college essay had now become a California state law Bella had sent emails urging University of Santa Clara and University of Portland Admissions to "turn on the news and see for yourself."

Both colleges responded immediately, congratulating Bella for the terrific accomplishment. Not only did they say they made a mistake by not admitting her to their colleges, but they both offered her admittance and pleaded that she choose their college.

For Bella, ProjectMerit made all the difference into getting into the college of her dreams. It is a project that gives college admissions a good glimpse of who you are. You are showing them what is worthwhile to you. You are giving them more than they asked for, but just what they want.

"People talk all the time about ideas they have for the world, but never do anything about them. You are going to be different."

This book is not a college or career guide. While college and career decisions should not be taken lightly, there are dozens of other books focusing on careers choices. This book is for students who have already thought carefully about the college they wish to attend and the career they would like to pursue and have decided that they will be best served at a highly selective college.

If you are ready for the next step, then you will need all the help you can get playing the college admissions game. This book will offer that help by showing you how to design and finish an independent project that will set you apart from other applicants. Your ideas are important, and have the potential to make the world a better place. People talk all the time about ideas they have for the world, but never do anything about them. You are going to be different. You are going to act on your ideas. You are going to start something, work on it very hard, and complete it.

History of the College Application Process

To help you understand how the college application process came to be and how it has changed significantly with the times, we briefly look back at a certain turning point in the US higher education history: The invention of the SAT test, an IQ test developed by Alfred Binet to measure a student's aptitude, or innate mental ability.

During the 1920's to 1960's, admissions tests became known as the main tool to accomplish and uniformity and objectivity. The first Scholastic Aptitude Test (SAT) was administered to the first group of college applicants in 1926. The test was intended to indicate a candidate's ability to successfully perform collegiate work. The American College Testing Program (ACT) test came around in 1959. Unlike the SAT, the ACT was administered to measure the extent to which the high school student had mastered college-related skills and knowledge.

As colleges became accustomed to the process of standardized testing as a measure of institutional quality the process became more competitive.

Colleges started looking at students who belonged to clubs and participated in team sports. They were interested in students who were involved in community service and students who held part-time jobs. As a result, high schools started to offer a larger variety of clubs and students began signing up for two, three or more of these clubs. Some high schools also began to require a certain number of hours of community service as part of their graduation requirements. In effect, colleges started to receive application forms that were spilling over with unbelievable numbers of hours committed to sports, community service and jobs. Stuffing activities into pages of college applications became the norm and admissions came to expect it.

Because college hopefuls joined the trend of actively participating in school clubs, sports, and community service, selective colleges began looking for students who had even more activity than the minimum high school requirements.

Nowadays, the validity of standardized testing is being challenged, and one of many reasons is because testing cannot possibly account for worthwhile skills the student may possess such as effective communication and responsible citizenship.

Hence the college essay was born. By the 1950's, most schools had adopted the requirement of a college essay: a brief personal statement of why the candidate had chosen to apply to one school over another. Students now write up to 500 words on the subject of themselves, including ethical dilemmas, public issues and creative influences. This will be your chance to talk about your project. This will be the time to show you in action.

Who do colleges want?

Rachel Toor, a former Duke University Admissions Officer, says that today's admissions officers are drawn to "angular kids, those with a much more focused interest or talent." What she means is that admissions officers are looking for students with the passion and initiative to start, develop and complete projects of their own. A student who has been working on a personal project over the entire duration of high school shows much more promise than one who simply followed a pre-existing pattern of required activity like being on the debate team for one semester.

"Colleges want a kid who is devoted to-and excels at-something. The word they most often use is passion," said Steve Cohen, co-author of "Getting In! The Zinch Guide to College Admissions and Financial Aid in the Digital Age" to the Washington Post.

Many colleges post their selection criteria on their websites so you can informally calculate how your application may rank. The University of California campuses, for example, consider 14 selection criteria in addition to minimum requirements in their admissions decisions. With each criteria weighted with a different number of points, they consider factors such as the strength of your school's curriculum, cumulative grades, test scores, student projects in academic areas, community involvement, special talents, leadership in cross-cultural activities, proficiency in other languages, rigor of the senior year, and overcoming adversity.

In addition, according to the National Association for College Admission Counseling (NACAC), as reported by researchers from the Department of Educational Administration (DEA), "colleges and universities use at least 12 specific admissions criteria (NACAC, February 2001). Admission criteria include: ability to pay, samples of written essays, interviews, recommendations from high school counselors and teachers, and evidence of exceptional leadership skills."

Each state is responsible for determining the minimum graduation requirements, however many states are similar. In California, for example, the minimum high school requirements for freshman admissions to California State Universities and University of California campuses include four years of English, three years of Mathematics, two (UC recommends three) years of Laboratory Sciences, two years of Social Studies/Sciences, two (UC recommends three) years of Foreign Language, one year of Visual/Performing Arts, and one year of electives from approved academic courses. Because you have chosen to attend a selective college, you will want to take the most challenging courses offered at your high school or even a few courses at your local college.

Some colleges use a formulaic process to select their incoming students, while others build a class by selecting students to assemble a well-balanced class (not to be confused with a well-balanced student). Among the colleges seeking a well-balanced class, a high-scoring student who excels in playing the clarinet may not be admitted simply because they're looking for a high-scoring student who excels in playing the oboe. This process will be out of your control. In order to even out its environment, some institutions may admit applicants simply to appeal to a narrower demographic. You may be applying to a mostly female college at a time when the school is at a tipping point. They need more males, and you happen to be among a small percentage of males with the qualifications.

Some colleges give special consideration to legacies (students whose parents or grandparents attended the same college) or under-represented groups in particular demographics and fields such as "women in engineering."

Check admissions criteria for each of the colleges you plan to apply to so you understand the process and know what each college considers important in the admissions game.

Remember, college admissions officers are much like corporate employee recruiters. What admissions committees want are students who can excel inside and outside of the high school setting, students who demonstrate originality, initiative, and leadership. Great colleges admit the students who show the potential to become the next Toni Morrison or Steve Jobs. When an influential person makes a mark in the world and the world finds out where she went to college, that college becomes even more desirable. Harvard Law became "THE" law school when the public learned President Obama graduated from there. When Harvard law is sifting through applications, you can rest assure they are looking to find someone who has the potential to be the next President.

Summary

Institutions are looking to determine which students have the most potential to be successful in college (and even more successful once they graduate four years later). College admissions officers are intent on building a class of incoming freshmen who are independent thinkers, natural leaders, and invested teachers with gifted, creative minds.

You will need to convince colleges that you have this level of talent and potential. The best way to do it is with an independent project—not your typical class project that consists of posters and presentations—but an original undertaking outside the classroom that encompasses your personal vision.

What could this project be? Ideally, your project should reflect something you are passionate about, which is also in line with your future aspirations.

"ProjectMERIT students have started their own businesses because they believe in a certain product, started non-profits because they have desires to change the world for the better, published books because of their creativity and love for the written word, produced films out of a desire to spread a message and conducted experiments to help preserve our planet for the future."

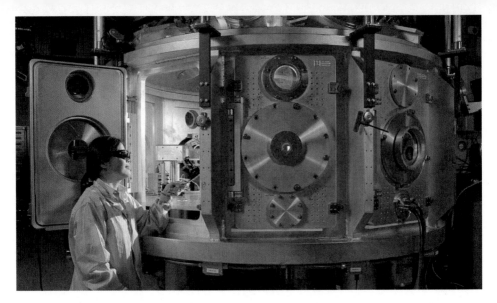

By using this book as a guide, you will have all you need to begin with your own idea. The easy-to-follow system will help you identify, organize, and complete your project. With enough motivation, you can do this on your own and get yourself into the college of your dreams.

CHAPTER I:
ProjectMERIT

What is a Project?

A high school project for a college-bound student is your great idea put into action. It will be the work outside of your school work that you have come up with to make your mark in the world. As your idea picks up momentum, you will have more insight into way the great wheel of progress works. Instead of going through the motions of high school, you will be one who creates change, who learns about the workings of the world, and ultimately, who grows up to be a useful member of the community.

First imagine yourself without boundaries. No one is standing there to tell you whether or not your ideas are good. It's time to brainstorm. Ask yourself what interests you. Make a list. Do you see any project ideas within that list?

A project can be the creation of an event, organization, business, publication, production/film, or experiment. Not to be confused with required class projects that consist simply of posters, videos, or presentations that must follow an outline the teacher has prepared for you, ProjectMerit is the culmination of your idea. You will be planning, producing, and presenting this original idea to the world, not to the teacher with the red pen.

This is not something your parents do with you side-by- side. You must figure this one out by yourself. You will meet with your parent or mentor on occasion for feedback, but in order to take on ProjectMerit you need to be prepared to do this on your own. We will talk about finding a mentor on page 59.

The ideal time to begin ProjectMerit is as early as 8th grade, or freshman year in high school. This project doesn't have to be in your future declared major, but it should be something you are curious about or engaged in. Take it as an opportunity to explore a career. The brainstorming process varies per person. Some of my students have decided on their project idea within a week and some have taken up to a year. Remember, this is not about pleasing your parents. This is about you. It is essential to select a project that you are very interested in because you are the one who will be intimately involved with this project for years – at least until high school graduation.

Real Examples of ProjectMerit
(Some names have been changed*)

Here are some ProjectMerit projects that helped these students get into college. As you brainstorm, think of ways that you can make a personal impact on the world.

Frank's Historical Novel
Frank* found his interest while delving into his family genealogy. He also loved to write. For his project, Frank chose to write a historical novel (based on his own family history) about the hardships of a family who was separated during WWII. By researching historical archives and reference materials and conducting interviews of family members, he collected enough

information for the historical accuracy of his novel. To help him form his characters, Frank worked with a university professor on understanding the social behavior in Japan during WWII. After completing his novel, Frank submitted it to publishers and to historical societies and museums for publication and endorsement. Frank now attends University of Southern California.

Nicole's Hydrogen Fuel Cell Experiment

Nicole's interests were in science and alternative energy. She started her project with an experiment to see if she could assemble a hydrogen fuel cell. She became one of the first students in the world to reach this goal. Nicole attended local meetings to learn about clean, sustainable energy and spent many hours studying alternatives to fossil fuel. She applied for a grant and won funding from the Department of Energy to work with research scientists at a California State University campus. She provided demonstrations of her very own hydrogen fuel cell at universities and conventions across the nation for four years and then gave speeches and told her story to more than 20 publications. Nicole has since published several articles of her own for industry magazines, organizations, and newspapers. Nicole graduated with honors in Neuroscience from Stanford University, completed medical school at Stanford School of Medicine, finished her residency at Harbor UCLA, and is currently doing an EMS fellowship at UC San Francisco.

Tom's Baseball Clinic

Tom had a passion for sports and a motivation to see all young people enjoy sports like he did. Having enjoyed the luxury of his own pitching machine in his backyard, he organized Saturday baseball clinics for a group of 25 low-income children. He began his project by asking his parents if he could use the family's pitching machine for the clinic. Next, he advertised his program by distributing brochures and posters at schools, Girls and Boys Club, YMCA, and public libraries. He sought out and won a sponsorship from the local Kiwanis Club to finance equipment and uniform purchases. Tom's clinic was well-received, and the story was told on the front page of the local newspaper. Tom earned a bachelor's degree from Santa Clara University and is now the CEO and founder of his own start-up.

Jaclyn's Non-Profit

Amidst the terrorism scare of 9/11 and the Iraq War, Jaclyn passionately vowed to change America's dependence on foreign energy. She researched viable alternatives and decided, for her project she would convert an internal combustion engine (ICE) to use gaseous hydrogen. Jaclyn selected a mentor who guided her as she launched her project. The experiment was a success. Jaclyn contacted the leading researchers in the industry to let them know she was an advocate for hydrogen fuel, and went to every hydrogen convention she could manage. Her project expanded when she started a non-profit organization, Kids 4 Hydrogen, to educate the public on hydrogen as an alternative to fossil fuel. She built a website to for educational outreach and wrote grants to finance the activism she was involved in. Jaclyn gave a speech at California Governor Arnold Schwarzenegger's Awards Ceremony and also spoke at the National Hydrogen Association Conference. During her project work she met with Senator Diane Feinstein and Congresswoman Anna Eshoo in Washington DC to promote Kids 4 Hydrogen. She graduated from Claremont McKenna College and received over $140,000 in scholarships. She is currently working on her MBA at the Kellogg School of Management at Northwestern University.

John's Short Film on Religion

A self-proclaimed movie critic, John* thought he would try his hand at making a film of his own. In response to America's resistance to teaching world religions in public schools, John wrote, directed and produced a satire on the world's five major religions. John extensively researched the doctrines and history of Christianity, Judaism, Buddhism, Islam, and Hinduism. Then he wrote his screenplay, had it reviewed, and revised it until it was ready. John ran auditions, set his cast, designed the sets, organized volunteers to build the sets and sew the costumes, and selected the music for his screenplay. After taking courses at the local community TV station, John was able to film the short at the TV station. Using their digital editing software, he edited the movie and copied it to DVDs. John plans to "shop" his movie to major motion picture studios. John earned a bachelor's degree from Columbia University and is now an independent filmmaker and political activist.

CHAPTER II:
Why do a Project?

Students who have completed ProjectMerit realize they have power in their thoughts and actions. They see something wrong or missing in the world, and make it right. ProjectMerit students are motivated to improve our quality of life, to protect our planet's natural resources, and to help people in our communities. Students who finish ProjectMerit become confident in the process, which in turn, makes them more successful in their careers.

Three Reasons to Start and Finish a Project

1) **To get into college**

The obvious answer to this question is that the college admissions officers will be more impressed with your application package if you have completed a comprehensive project on your own. You'll have the opportunity to tell them what you have done to demonstrate your passion, drive, leadership, tenacity, and follow-through. This is quite a feat in comparison to most other college applicants. While most students will write about their dream to do something meaningful someday in their personal statements, you will be writing about how you have already accomplished a dream.

2) To make good use of your time

There is another reason to do a project: Now is the best time to start pursuing your dreams. Although you might not fully appreciate it at this time, teenagers have a luxury that disappears as they enter the adult world. As a teenager, you might have to pay for your gas, but you probably don't have to worry about working to pay the rent or to buy your groceries, and you probably don't have a spouse to support or children to take care of. While becoming an adult certainly doesn't end your freedoms, it might reduce the amount of time you can devote to your own personal pursuits. You might never have the chance to do a project like this again, so take advantage of this opportunity!

3) To make the world a better place

Projects (of the ProjectMerit kind) make the world a better place for all of us. While other teenagers are spending their time worrying about what clothes to wear, who to hang out with, or who is on Facebook, instead you can do something that makes a difference. If every student completed ProjectMerit in high school, imagine how many social, political, and environmental problems would be solved! Imagine how much compassion we would have for one another! Imagine the justice that would be served and the barriers that would fall!

CHAPTER III:
Getting Started

First and foremost, you need to decide on the theme of your project. Because this project will span over several years, you don't want to be stuck doing something that you are not interested in. This choice is important. While it may seem like everything good has already been done, it is perfectly fine to put a modern twist on an idea that has been out for a while and needs an update. The goal is to do a project that interests you and at the same time, improves society.

Consider local as well as global issues. Read newspapers and magazines. Watch the news on TV or online. Discuss what's going on in the community, nation, and world with friends, teachers, co-workers, or family. Don't worry about the magnitude of the problems as you make a list of possibilities. Having boundaries limits the decision-making process. You will know when you have found your project. It will have to be something that you care about. It will be something that either gets you upset and then excited or creatively charged and then excited. Few things motivate us better than our passions. Think about the things you find to be unjust. Think about the times when you said, "If only there was an invention that could..." Think about the times you read a news article and felt outraged or saw something on the news that got you all riled up.

Begin by asking yourself these questions as you brainstorm about possible project topics: (You can highlight issues that pique your interest)

1. **Which problems exist at your school? (Partially listed in the National Center for Education Statistics)**
   - Alcohol use
   - Bullying
   - Cliques
   - Drug use
   - Gang violence
   - Lack of counseling resources
   - Lack of creative options/classes- Art (art supplies), Music (music instruments), Dance (dance room), Drama (theatre space), Video production (video production equipment)
   - Lack of foreign language classes- Instruction, Materials
   - Lack of life science options- Garden space, Farming tools, Seed & soil
   - Lack of parental involvement
   - Lack of physical activities- P.E., Equipment, After-school sports
   - Lack of recycling/environmental options- Reducing, Reusing, Recycling
   - Lack of science options- Lab equipment, Science instruction, Science Fair
   - Lack of technology- Computers, Video equipment
   - Low test scores
   - Parental alcoholism
   - Poor nutritional choices- Cafeteria, Vending machines, Lunches from home, Low-income free lunch program

- Poverty
- Student apathy
- Student absenteeism
- Run-down/unsafe campus grounds- Mold, ADA violations, Bike racks, Buildings, Landscape, Parking lot
- Weapons possession
- Other

2. Which problems exist in your community?
   - Animal abuse
   - Dangerous roads/buildings
   - Drug/Alcohol Abuse- DUIs, DWIs
   - Education- Low-achieving schools
   - Environmental issues
   - Homelessness
   - Lack of after-school activities for children- Recreation centers, Basketball courts, Swimming pools
   - Lack of benefits in the workplace
   - Unemployment
   - Lack of aesthetic beauty- Public art, Natural surroundings, Architecture
   - Lack of courtesy/human connection- volunteerism
   - Lack of fun things to do
   - Lack of (good) parks for children- Run-down/ neglected parks
   - Lack of health insurance

- Lack of affordable healthy/fresh food in the stores- Farmer's markets, Organic options
- Lack of places to exercise- Bike trails, Hiking trails, Running and walking paths, Sidewalks
- Lack of public festivals- Music, Dance, Art, Seasonal, Holiday
- Lack of variety in businesses- Empty buildings
- Legal injustice
- Low/unfair salaries in the workplace
- Poor parenting
- Poor public libraries- Hours, Staff, Children's programs, Computers
- Poverty
- Prejudice
- Sexism
- Violence/ crime
- Other

3. **Which political issues get you "fired-up?"**
   - Defense/ Security- Military spending, Treatment of veterans, UN (International affairs)
   - Distribution of wealth
   - Economic development- growth of income, long-term planning
   - Education- Literacy, Public schools, Private schools, Charter schools, Alternative education, Funding
   - Famine/Hunger- Charitable giving, Philanthropy

- Financial- Credit card companies, Credit scores, National/personal debt, Stock market, Small business, Corporations
- Gambling
- Gas Prices
- Government institutions- CIA, FBI, DMV, IRS, EDD, Congress
- Government programs- Medicare, Welfare, Family Leave, Maternity Leave
- Green development
- Health care- Affordability, Quality
- Housing- Foreclosures, Homelessness, Bank loans
- Human Rights- Abortion, Same-sex marriage, Women's rights, Racial equality
- Immigration- Obtaining citizenship, Deportation, Justice, Prejudice
- Law and justice- Court System, Local & State laws
- Lobbying- Pork barrel and Ear mark spending
- Peace- civic activism, non-violence
- Political campaigns- Voting
- Prisons- Juvenile hall, Maximum security, Death penalty, Three Strikes, Alternatives
- Privacy- Surveillance, Stalking, Witness Protection, Internet
- Religion in politics
- Short-term economic planning
- Sustainable agriculture

- Taxation
- Torture
- Social Security
- Unemployment- Job opportunities
- War
- Other

4. **Which social issues interest you?**

- Ageism/ Youth rights
- Age of consent
- Alcohol laws
- Bullying
- Capital Punishment
- Censorship
- Corporal punishment
- Corruption
- Domestic violence/rape
- Drug laws
- Gambling laws
- Gun rights
- Homophobia
- Immigration
- Old Age
- Panhandling
- Poverty
- Prostitution laws
- Racism
- Riots

- Same-sex marriage
- School leaving age
- Sexism
- Suicide and Assisted suicide
- Terrorism
- Tobacco and smoking laws
- Traffic
- Unemployment
- Welfare of children- foster-care, adoption, child abuse, child molestation, child abduction, child labor, child poverty, child obesity
- Other

5. **Which health and wellness topics interest you?**
   - AIDS
   - Alcohol abuse
   - Allergies
   - Alternative healing
   - Autism
   - Bone health
   - Cancer
   - Diabetes
   - Diseases/epidemics- rare, common, prevention
   - Drug abuse
   - Energy work
   - Fitness
   - Food industry
   - Food share programs
   - Genetically-modified foods

- Heart Disease
- Local, sustainable foods
- Pharmaceuticals
- Massage/body work
- Meditation
- Mental Illness
- Nutrition (organic foods, raw foods, vegetarianism/veganism, diets, fads, calories)
- Obesity
- Organic farming
- Pesticides on crops
- Smoking
- Vitamins/ supplements
- Other

6. **Which of these environmental issues (from Wikipedia. com) interest you?**
   - Climate Change- global warming, global dimming, fossil fuels, sea level rise, greenhouse gas, ocean acidification, shutdown of thermohaline circulation, environmental impact of the coal industry, Urban Heat Islands)
   - Conservation- species extinction, pollinator decline, coral bleaching, Holocene extinction, invasive species, poaching, endangered species
   - Energy- energy conservation, renewable energy, efficient energy use, renewable energy commercialization, environmental impact of the coal industry

- Environmental degradation- Eutrophication, Habitat destruction, invasive species
- Environmental health- air quality, Asthma, environmental impact of the coal industry, electromagnetic fields, electromagnetic radiation and health, indoor air quality, lead poisoning, Sick Building Syndrome
- Genetic engineering- Genetic pollution, Genetically modified food controversies
- Intensive farming- Overgrazing, Irrigation, Monoculture, environmental effects of meat production, slash and burn, pesticide drift, plasticulture
- Land degradation- Land pollution, Desertification

    Soil- Soil conservation, Soil erosion, Soil contamination, Soil salination
- Land use- Urban sprawl, Habitat fragmentation, Habitat destruction
- Nanotechnology- Nanotoxicology, Nanopollution
- Nuclear issues- Nuclear fallout, Nuclear meltdown, Nuclear power, Nuclear weapons, Nuclear and radiation accidents, Nuclear safety, High-level radioactive waste management
- Overpopulation- Burial, water crisis, Overpopulation in companion animals, Tragedy of the commons, Gender Imbalance in Developing Countries, Sub-replacement fertility levels in developed countries

- Ozone depletion- CFC, Biological effects of UV exposure
- Pollution- Environmental impact of the coal industry, Nonpoint source pollution, Point source pollution, Light pollution, Noise pollution, Visual Pollution

  Water pollution- Environmental impact of the coal industry, Acid rain, Eutrophication, Marine pollution, Ocean dumping, Oil spills, Thermal pollution, Urban runoff, Water crisis, Marine debris, Microplastics, Ocean acidification, Ship pollution, Wastewater, Fish kill, Algal bloom, Mercury in fish

  Air pollution- Environmental impact of the coal industry, Smog, Tropospheric ozone, Indoor air quality, Volatile organic compound, Atmospheric particulate matter
- Reservoirs- Environmental impacts of reservoirs
- Resource depletion- Exploitation of natural resources, Overdrafting

  Consumerism- Consumer capitalism, Planned obsolescence, Over-consumption

  Fishing- Blast fishing, Bottom trawling, Cyanide fishing, Ghost nets, Illegal, unreported and unregulated fishing, Overfishing, Shark finning, Whaling

  Logging- Clearcutting, Deforestation, Illegal logging

  Mining- Acid mine drainage, Hydraulic

fracturing, Mountaintop removal mining, Slurry impoundments

- *Toxins- Chlorofluorocarbons, DDT, Endocrine disruptors, Dioxin, Toxic heavy metals, Environmental impact of the coal industry, Herbicides, Pesticides, Toxic waste, PCB, Bioaccumulation, Biomagnification*
- *Waste- Electronic Waste, Litter, Waste disposal incidents, Marine debris, Medical waste, Landfill, Leachate, Environmental impact of the coal industry, Incineration, Great Pacific Garbage Patch, Exporting of hazardous waste*

Most students spend a good amount of time brainstorming about topics for their projects. With the magnitude of this undertaking, a student may take up to a year to finally select a project that suits their personality and interests.

Good ideas don't always pop up during your first brainstorming session. Jaclyn didn't wake up one morning with a revelation that she would start Kids 4 Hydrogen, yet she did know that she was passionate about the solution of environmental issues, especially those involving renewable energy.

The metamorphosis of her project idea took place over a 10-month span. She attended several conventions and researched all of the major alternative energy possibilities, including solar, wind, geothermal, and biomass energy.

She met with a mentor who had worked at NASA to brainstorm the latest developments in alternative energy. Her mentor helped develop several leads. Jaclyn then organized a brainstorming meeting on alternative energy, inviting 20 scientists (both active and retired) for a four-hour think-tank session.

During the meeting, she became interested in news about the latest developments in making fuel from alcohol. Jaclyn spent the next eight months making mash from fruit stock, building a still, and working with government officials to clear the way for her to legally produce fuel from alcohol she produced herself. It wasn't until she "did the math" (and realized how much stock was needed to produce the necessary quantities to satisfy America's energy consumption) that she decided alcohol fuel would not be sustainable. Back to the drawing board, the process took time to learn about hydrogen's importance in the energy future. After those ten months of study and debate, however, Jaclyn was ready to start a non-profit for the promotion hydrogen fuel.

Tom*, on the other hand, picked his project in one week. He wanted to do something that would give him the ability to spend every free minute (when he wasn't doing homework) doing something that had to do with baseball.

When he arrived to practice early one day, he observed a Little League coach working with his team. The coach was only working with a few of the top players while ignoring the less-talented of the bunch. This made Tom angry. He could see that the other players had potential but might never have the change to improve their game. Tom had the luxury of having his own batting cages at home and private coaches to give him baseball pointers. He thought, Why shouldn't these kids have an the same opportunity? Tom knew in an instant just what his community needed to provide for these young players, and his project was born.

For help with brainstorming for your project, visit **www. meritworld.com** to talk to a Merit online college advisor. Find examples of more student projects in the Project Gallery link.

CHAPTER IV:
Research: Is Your Idea Viable?

The first thing you set your mind on may not be the best choice for your project. Even if you have a favorite activity and think you know exactly what your project should be, you still need to hold a brainstorming session with your parents, teachers or friends.

An idea that seems perfect to you might sound different to other people. Don't be afraid to let others help you see things from another angle. A fresh look may show you the holes in your idea, or may offer great thoughts on how to improve it, or move it in a more exciting direction. Keep in mind that no one is asking you to save the planet single-handedly. However, if you have found your niche (and have an idea you think you can follow through with) you will find the help you need to make it happen.

Perhaps you have several ideas for your project. Make a list of your ideas. Start with number one and run it through a search engine like Google. This may sound simple, but first you need to find out if your idea has already been done. If your project consists of experimentation or discovery (as in patenting a product) then there is a possibility that it may already be available to the public.

You may need to cross some of your ideas of the list when you find it already exists in the capacity you would like to see it. Or you may find your idea is out there in the world, and is similar to yours, but after some inquiry, you find improvements or innovations could be made.

Let's say your biggest concern is caring for the low and medium-income families in your community. On the top of your list is:

1. Providing free food to local people who are struggling to make ends meet

You type in "Free food Santa Cruz County" in a search engine. Alas, you find that Santa Cruz County soup kitchens already offer daily meals to homeless people every day in many locations. You decide your energy may be better served by finding a specific niche that may have been overlooked by the soup kitchens or other organizations.

For example, you discover local soup kitchens are only available for the homeless and food pantries and food stamps are only available for low-income families. You have been bothered by the stories you hear about medium-income families who have homes and are working as much as they possibly can, but have little money for food after the high cost of living. You start to think of food programs for medium-income families that provides food for when they experience tough times or rough patches. You continue researching ideas other communities have come up with in regards to providing food for those who need it. You hear of one city that started a free farm stand for anyone who needs it and another that organized anonymous grocery bag deliveries with all the essentials. You come up with an idea that is a combination of the two, but with your personal touch: a food stand and food delivery service for low-medium income community members that also maintains the receiver's dignity by offering "service coupons" to pay back for the food in labor services.

Now that you have a good project idea, it is time to make some phone calls to organizations, agencies or businesses that relate to what you are doing. This will help you learn more about your subject and it may also develop opportunities for partnership in the future. Make a list of questions before you call. You will need to ask about their goals, their audience (who they serve), and their structure. Take notes while you talk on the phone (or if they can meet with you in person- even better). Keep your notes in a binder with your project ideas.

At this point you will have a much better understanding of your subject. It is time to decide whether or not the community has a need for your project. If you found that there are one or more groups already doing exactly what you had in mind to set up, you either need to go back to the drawing board to find a new project, or you will need to change the focus of your project so you are not duplicating efforts. Consider the following questions while doing your preliminary research:

1. *What will my project accomplish?*
2. *How can I fine tune my project to make it original?*
3. *How can I fine tune my project so I can accomplish my goal by the time I graduate from high school?*
4. *Is there a special niche market for my project?*
5. *What other programs or organizations are doing similar things?*
6. *Is there room for my project, or will I be duplicating other efforts?*
7. *Would my project compliment the work of existing programs or organizations?*
8. *Would I appeal to a new audience?*
9. *How are other programs structured? Who do they service? How are they financed? Who conducts the work? Who leads the effort? How do they recruit volunteers?*
10. *Is there another direction I should explore?*

Once you establish that your idea is viable – that there is a need and other existing programs won't interfere with your project, then you can brainstorm your goals and how to meet them.

For example, if your project is to match senior citizens with young children to promote reading literacy, then you will need to set up a recruitment program for seniors interested in working with children for a few hours a day, find a suitable location, select the students who would benefit from your program, purchase reading materials and equipment, and set up a marketing plan. As you explore similar programs or operations, make a list of services you would like to offer.

Select a Name for Your Project, Organization, or Business

It's best to pick a name that is easily understandable and sums up what your mission is, as opposed to some overly technical name or some obscure acronym. For instance, Kids 4 Hydrogen clearly states that this organization consist of kids who support hydrogen fuel. Other names like The D'Arcy Foundation or ABC don't tell the public what they do. Check to make sure that another organization isn't using the same or similar name. If you plan to use an acronym like TEAM (Teens Educating At-Risk Minors), a name created by the initials of the company name, do an online search to ensure that the acronym isn't already being used. You don't want any embarrassing surprises initiated by confusion about your name.

Create a logo for your organization that projects the kind of image you want. The logo is the first thing that many people will use to form an impression of your organization. If you want to project a high-tech image, the logo shouldn't be cartoonish, but a cartoonish logo would be good if the project deals with young children. Narrow fonts suggest understated sophistication, while wide fonts suggest power. A plain white or pastel background suggests purity, and would be good for an ecological cause.

Using clipart or graphics software can be an easy way to design your logo, or you could enlist the help of an artistic friend. You can even simply use fonts to create your logo. For instance, IBM is a worldwide logo that is recognized simply by its font. Other logos such as Apple, uses a symbol – the apple with a bite taken out of it, and Nike uses the swoosh symbol. When using fonts, make sure that they can easily be read or that your slogan clarifies or restates it. For example, Peterson Company doesn't indicate what the company sells or what types of services it provides.

Many companies and organizations use slogans or taglines to further describe their missions. Rocket Juice adds "Nutrition for your Mission" as its slogan. Volvo adds "Powered for Life" to reach its customer base. Slogans are usually written below the logo and business name and they are in smaller or italicized letters. A good slogan or tagline should say a little more about what your project is, without being too long, but should also be catchy. To make your slogan catchy, use a poetic device like alliteration or rhyme.

The Plan: Fine-Tuning the Scope of the Project

Whether you're out to redefine America's energy source, open a school of robotics, patent a wireless device, or market a new breakfast cookie, you'll need to fine tune and outline the entire scope of your project. It's important at this stage to narrow your project down to something that you can realistically do in just a few years. While your heart may want you to find a cure for AIDS and stop its spread in Africa, realistically, you won't be able to do that by the time you graduate from high school. But, you can create an organization that solicits donations to buy AIDS medication for millions suffering with AIDS in Africa. Or, you could become an advocate pushing for pharmaceutical companies to develop a generic brand of medications that can be used in Africa. Or, you can set up educational outreach programs aimed at a particular group, for instance, African teens. Find the country or region with the most AIDS victims, and target outreach or medical support in that area. By fine tuning your project, you'll be able to better manage its successful completion.

Hannah first decided to put together a photo journal of hot spots around the world for teens. Bored with family vacations, she thought that teens would appreciate a guide that shows where they could escape from the drudgery of touring museums with their families and find the best places to eat, meet other kids, and have fun. While this was a great idea, Hannah was a junior and only had 10 months to select and complete her project. So, instead of covering hundreds of cities worldwide, she decided to focus on San Francisco, her hometown. This was considerably easier because she already knew all of the best places to get dim sum or pizza. Getting photographs of her friends shopping in Union Square was fun. With her camera, she captured teens riding bikes or skating in Golden Gate Park on Sundays, when cars were banned, visiting the famous wax museum, and eating clam chowder in a sourdough bread bowl. By fine-tuning her original idea, Hannah's San Francisco photo journal guide book for teens was completed just in time for her to write about it in her personal statement.

Consider the following:

1. Will you need to recruit volunteers? Will you post fliers, contact high school counselors, or place an ad in high school papers?

2. Who will finance your materials costs? (See Setting Up a Budget on page 62) Can you get local businesses to donate their services or products or money?

3. Can you really complete your project in the time you have left in high school? Can you reduce your plan to make it more manageable?

4. How will you inform the public about your project? Will you contact the press? Political leaders? Industry leaders?

5. What geographical areas will you involve?

6. What hours will you be of service?

Setting up a Timeline and Laying Out Milestones

First, you'll need a calendar that includes all of the months until your high school graduation (you may need to go online to print this out) to layout general project milestones; details will be entered in your planner later. Enter the project completion date (in pencil) on the August before your senior year. Your project needs to be up and running or completed before the start of 12th grade. This will give you the opportunity to address your project in your college application essays that you will write in August to December of your senior year.

In chronological order, make a list of general goals. For example, if your project is to convert a gasoline engine to use gaseous hydrogen, your general goals might look something like this:

1. Create your organization: name, logo, mission statement, fliers, website
2. Meet with industry leaders to discuss your project
3. Make sponsor kits
4. Write grant
5. Apply for non-profit status
6. Purchase car (get one donated: send fliers to dealers, manufacturers, repair shops)
7. Work with mentor (industry leader) to convert your car
8. Organize nationwide tour (universities, auto mechanic tech schools, energy conferences, Washington DC)
9. Contact media about tour (TV talk shows, radio talk shows, industry magazines, local newspapers)
10. Update website (conversion process, list of sponsors, grants received)
11. Complete tour (document tour with photos, letters of recommendation from sponsors, copies of press)
12. Update website (photos of tour)

For a literary project, like writing historical fiction, your general goals might look something like this:

1. Write an outline of the plot (include major historical events and story line)
2. Develop a list and description of characters (include characters that represent characteristics specific to the period)
3. Describe settings
4. Divide the outline into chapters
5. Decide the time needed to write each chapter and list deadlines for each
6. Estimate the number of months needed to write the novel (include time for research)
7. Select editors to read and critique the novel
8. Select illustrator (if needed)
9. Edit novel 5-10 times (each read-through should be separated by at least a week; this process will take several months, especially if working with an editor)
10. Set up timeline of historical events for novel
11. Make 10 copies of your manuscript
12. Write query letter to publishers
13. Send query letter with table of contents and sample chapter to publishers
14. At their request, send full manuscript to publishers
15. Negotiate publisher's contract
16. Write marketing plan for your novel
17. Contact history curriculum planners and conventions to get endorsement for your novel

Planning Tasks

If you don't use an appointment book or planner, go out and get one. Even if you think you're organized and can remember everything you need to do to successfully complete a project while going to school, participating in extracurricular activities, and hanging out with friends, you'll need a planner to help you stay on top of all of your responsibilities. You could purchase appointment books at stationary stores or you can order Merit's Academic Planners (**www.meritworld.com**). You'll want a planner that is 8 ½" x 11" and opens out to a full week, including equal space for all seven days. Many appointment books minimize the space for Saturdays and Sundays, but your weekends will be just as important as your weekdays. Planners that start early in the morning and end at midnight are ideal.

Now it's time to super-organize your life. If time management or organization has not been a priority in your life, you may need to rethink how you spend your days. Before you started this project and possibly before you started to get serious about college admissions, frankly, you didn't really need to manage your time. Your teachers probably gave you homework assignments that were due the following day – taking the need out of planning ahead because the teachers planned out each step for the completion of your big project or papers for you. Rather than giving you a practice and game schedule for the entire athletic season, your coach probably mentioned the date and time of your next practice or game as you headed out of the locker room each day. And, instead of giving you your household list of weekly, or monthly, chores, your parents probably asked, or nagged, you to empty the dishwasher or take out the trash just as you were heading out the door.

Life is not going to be as simple anymore. Homework, after-school activities, and chores need to be handled well and efficiently in order for you to have enough time to complete your project. That doesn't mean that you have to become an antisocial recluse, but in order to accomplish your regular things, have time to do weekly tasks for your project, and have a social life, you're going to have to better manage your time.

Now that you have defined the scope of your project and you've outlined your project milestones on a calendar, it's time to lay out a plan to ensure that those milestones are met.

Make sure that you've entered in your classes, after-school activities, and chores for the rest of the semester/year in your planner, if you haven't done that, do it now. You never know when someone is going to ask you to speak or do a demonstration, and you want to be able to open your planner to see your schedule in a glance. Next, enter each homework assignment on the day it's due and when you plan to do them.

By looking at your calendar filled with milestones, it's time to set up specific tasks for each one. Starting with your first milestone, make a list of all steps needed to reach your goal. Then prioritize this list. Consider everything, even things like brainstorming about the name or slogan for your organization. It's best to micro-manage each activity to ensure that you have allowed enough time to get the job done. In your planner, enter these tasks around your homework and other commitments. By writing down each task, it acts as a reminder to you to make the call or do the work. As you get started, you'll need to update your planner as you go because you'll have to deal with unforeseen obstacles that may require another step.

If you're doing an internet search, you can plan to do this at the end of your night after you finish your homework. For example, if your general goal is to create a website for your organization, then your tasks might look something like this:

1. *Feb. 1: 4:00 pm: Call Josh to get the name of his web-design software and web-hosting service.*
2. *Feb. 2: 9:00 pm: Go online and compare other web-design programs and web-hosts.*
3. *Feb. 3: 3:00 pm: Sign up with web-hosting service.*
4. *Feb. 3: 9:00 pm: Order web-design software.*
5. *Feb. 4: 1:00 pm: Call friends and family for help with building your website*
6. *Feb. 5: 9:00 pm: Lay out the navigational structure your website. How many pages? What titles for each page? What links on each page?*
7. *Feb. 6: 9:00 pm: Write the text for page 1 and edit it.*
8. *Feb. 7: 9:00 pm: Write the text for page 2 and edit it.*
9. *Feb. 8: 9:00 pm: Write the text for page 3 and edit it.*
10. *Feb. 9: 9:00 pm: Write the text for page 4 and edit it.*
11. *Feb. 10: 9:00 pm: Select photos for website*
12. *Feb. 11: 9:00 pm: Discuss layout of page with friends (Buttons, background, colors)*
13. *Feb. 12: 4:00 pm: Call Josh to see if he could help you lay out your website now that you've received the software program.*
14. *Feb. 13: 10:00 am: Review text and ask English teacher to check for grammar and mechanical problems.*

15. *Feb. 14: 9:00 Edit photos*
16. *Feb. 15: 5:00 pm Create website with Josh (framework)*
17. *Feb. 16: 5:00 pm Check links and upload website.*
18. *Feb. 17: 9:00 pm Check your website. Correct any errors with links or text.*

Finding a Mentor: Someone Who is an Expert in This Field

It's important to establish your working relationship with the mentor at the start of the project. Nobody expects you to do this project alone. Your mentor will point you in the right direction so you don't waste time and won't get discouraged. As a matter of fact, the most successful projects are usually guided by professionals. Just because you have a mentor doesn't mean that you are the mentor's assistant or that it's their project. All you need to do is take control of the project and meet with your mentor for advice and guidance. Your mentor should not do all your research or conduct the experiment or program on your behalf.

A good mentor is someone who is either active in the field or who has had an active career in the field. If your project is specialized, then they should have the expertise to work with your specialization. Depending on your specific project, it may be difficult to find a mentor who is currently active and willing to work with you, not because they don't want to but simply because they may not have time. However, if your project will help an active professional with their career goals, your request for support may provide a mutually beneficial relationship. In many cases, you may not be able to find an active professional.

Don't despair though. Retired professionals are often ideal mentors because they have both the expertise and the available time. Call your local college and inquire about emeritus or retired professors.

Mention your plan to seek a mentor to your friends and family – they may have leads for you, or they can at least spread the word, and it could eventually get around to someone who may be helpful for you. The best place to start is with people you already know. Talk to your teachers, counselors, friends, parents of friends, and your parents. Even if they don't have expertise in the field, they may know someone who does. Learning to network with people you know is an invaluable skill. With networking, you'll learn to establish reputable connections in your community of friends, family, and associates. You'll get a lead from a friend that may turn into another lead. Most likely, you'll make important contacts and find your mentor through networking.

If networking, however, doesn't work for you, check industry publications to find the leading experts. Read their bios online to learn more about their history and the projects they are currently vested in. Check your local college to seek out professors, graduate students, or undergraduates who are working in your areas of interest. When working with undergraduate college mentors, check to make sure that they have both the expertise needed and the time to coach you. You can also discuss your project with industry magazines for leads. This process may take several months and you may hear many rejections before you find the right mentor. Enter in your planner all calls that you need to make so you stay focused on your search. Although making these cold calls may feel awkward at first, remember, the worst thing that could happen is that someone may say that they can't work with you. If you write an outline or a script to follow, you'll probably be more comfortable making your first phone calls. You can also write letters or send emails to inquire about mentoring.

Once you find the person who you think will make an ideal mentor, write a formal letter of request. In your letter, state your purpose, describe your project, praise the mentor's career accomplishments, and layout a general schedule proposal. If your sponsor or press kit is ready, include it with the letter. It's best to send a formal letter through the mail to make your initial contact and request. This will set the tone for your relationship so the mentor understands that you are looking for a professional and serious mentor. Once you start working with the mentor, email and phone correspondence will probably be your best mode of communication.

Tom found his mentor after getting his original lead from his high school chemistry teacher. His teacher recommended her neighbor, a retired chemist. Unfortunately, the retired chemist was moving out of state to live with his daughter so he couldn't guarantee that he would be able to consistently help Tom as his mentor. The retired chemist then gave Tom a few names of colleagues who were also retired. After calling all of the leads, Tom finally found a chemist who could guide him through his project.

Debbie researched activists who were fighting transgenic produce by doing a Google search. After checking their bios, she mailed them a formal letter outlining her concerns and describing her project. She found two mentors who gladly shared with her their history with their mission and the recent breakthroughs they've made. One of her mentors gave her inside information about the biggest pushers of transgenic produce and helped her organize her campaign to stop transgenic production of foods Americans eat.

Setting up a Budget

In order to determine how much money you'll need for your project, you'll need to lay out a budget. Sponsors who finance your project, those who provide your funding will request a proposed budget. They'll want to make sure that you understand what it will cost to complete the project. Imagine what would happen if you ran out of money half way through your project and couldn't finish it? Everybody involved with your project will want to be assured that you have thought out the budget and secured necessary funds. Make phone calls and look online to inquire about fees and costs. Lay out your budget using a spreadsheet program. You don't want to just start paying for the expenses as you go without understanding the full scope of your financial needs. When calculating each expense, over estimate your costs or add a 10% buffer to cover unexpected changes in your costs. Use the following categories when putting together your budget:

1. *Office Expenses (paper, envelopes, printer ink cartridges, press/sponsor kit, etc.)*
2. *Office Equipment (answering machine, phone, etc.)*
3. *Computer Equipment (computer, printer, software, etc.)*
4. *Phone (long distance calls)*

5. Postage (stamps, bulk mail permits and fees)
6. Website costs (monthly web-hosting fees, software costs, etc)
7. Project Costs (materials, equipment, rentals, etc.)
8. Travel Expenses (flights, gas, hotel, meals)
9. Exhibitor Fees (convention fees)
10. Consultant Fees (mentor fees, if necessary)

Select a Weekly Meeting w/Mentor or Self to Move Project Forward

With your busy school and extracurricular demands, your project will most likely get pushed aside, postponed, or even forgotten if you don't make it a regular part of your routine. If you're working with a mentor, set up a regular schedule to meet every week or two weeks. Naturally, other obligations may require that you change your regular meeting time, but having a regular schedule ensures that even if things get hectic one week, you'll still be on track the following week. Enter these meeting times in your planner for the duration of the year.

Even if you know that you're meeting with your mentor every Tuesday night and that this is something you don't think you need to write down, you still should. Once your project gets going and once you factor in all your other obligations, it's too easy to overlook your weekly meetings. Here are few sad stories about students who didn't organize their meetings with their mentors.

Matt used to be the whiz kid that everybody relied on for organizing everything from ski trips to planning class projects. After he started his project, he began to forget everything, from insignificant things like feeding the dog, to more relevant things like forgetting meetings with his mentor. It wasn't until he missed an important meeting with his mentor, who then decided to stop working with him, that Matt realized he needed a better system to organize his busy life.

Lori actually never finished her project. She selected a mentor but she didn't set a regular schedule and only met with him once every couple of months. The mentor lost interest in the project, and so did Lori.

Make Sponsor Kit to Get Someone to Finance and Endorse the Project

A Sponsor Kit is a packet filled with information about your project and you that you give to potential donors. It is typically filled with lots of statistics, photos, and contact information displayed in a professional layout to encourage the potential sponsor to finance a portion or the entire project. In addition to the content, the way the materials are presented is also important because presentation can make an enormous impact on potential sponsors. If the sponsor kit looks professional, those who read it will see that you're a responsible student who should be taken seriously. If the Sponsor Kit looks sloppy, then you might not be taken as seriously. Think of the Sponsor Kit as the instrument that demonstrates how capable and professional you are.

A typical Sponsor Kit may have any of the following items:
1. *Mission Statement (purpose of your project; who will benefit, who will do the work)*
2. *Budget (proposed detailed budget)*
3. *Biography and/or Resume (provide information about your education, athletics, clubs, volunteer work, jobs, awards, scholarships, publications, other projects, interests)*

4. *List of other Sponsors (encourages sponsors to do their part in supporting students)*
5. *Photo Sheet with Captions (display photos of your project, demonstrations, politicians, community leaders, speeches, community service)*
6. *Publications (select articles written by or about you, essays or research papers related to your project, or press releases)*

The Sponsor Kits can be as simple or as elaborate as your budget dictates. Some students use glossy pocket and 3-hole-punched folders, while others use inexpensive double pocket folders. If you have a lot of information to include in your Sponsor Kit, use dividers with tabs to make it easy to see at a glance the contents of the kit. Most word processor programs come preloaded with templates that make it easy to quickly create professional-looking documents. You can also cut each sheet of paper one inch shorter than the previous sheet to create a staircase effect. Use bold colors and make sure the text is easy to read. If you have a logo and slogan, place it on each section and on each sheet of paper. You want your project to stand out and to be remembered. Print out a full-page label with your project name, logo, slogan, and the title "Sponsor Kit," then stick it to the front.

When to make a Sponsor Kit can be a tricky question. Ideally, you want the Sponsor Kit ready at the start of your project so you can get funding right away. But, unless you've started the project and show promise, a potential sponsor may want to see your project further along before they commit to offering funding. I recommend making the Sponsor Kit after you've selected your project, calculated your budget, found a mentor, and laid out your plan of action in your planner. Then, as you reach new milestones, you can add new pages to your Sponsor Kit.

Prepare a handful of Sponsor Kits before you begin seeking financial assistance. Distribute the Sponsor Kits at conventions, seminars, or meetings that focus on your industry or subject matter. Call philanthropists who are interested in your project to ask if you can send them your kit. Always include a formal cover letter when sending Sponsor Kits. The cover letter should be customized to each individual sponsor, so you do not appear to be blanketing them with a mass-mailing. Even though each cover letter is customized, you can reuse much of the text from one to the next. Requests for financial support are better received when they are personalized and backed with a professional Sponsor Kit.

Sponsor Kits can also be used to get an endorsement for your project. By getting a public official, research scientist, or industry leader to endorse your project, you'll establish more credibility with sponsors and within your community. To request an endorsement, simply write a cover letter that introduces your project and request the endorsement, and include your Sponsor Kit. After you receive endorsements, add their letters of support or photos with you to your Sponsor Kit.

Make Press Kits to Introduce Your Project in Your Town

Press Kits are quite similar to Sponsor Kits, except for a few differences. Press Kits omit the budget and include all of the information the media will need to cover your project. A Press Release is an information sheet that usually accompanies the Press Kit. A Press Release includes information about your news after it has happened. If you're trying to get the press to cover your upcoming event, send them a News Advisory. The News Advisory is distributed to the press before the event to give them an early alert, with the hope that they'll cover your story. This includes the dates you will appear in public to debut or demonstrate your project. State whether you are inviting the press to your event or if you're asking them to simply announce the event. Include important details that the public will need to know: dates, times, costs, and locations, etc. Also, state when the News Advisory is ready for release. For instance, if you want to have the newspaper announce your event on a specific date, then write: News Advisory: For release on February 22. If you want the News Advisory to go out as soon as possible, then state: For Immediate Release.

A Press Kit is a packet filled with information about your project and you that you give to the media: TV, radio, magazines, and newspapers. It is typically filled with lots of statistics, photos, and contact information displayed in a professional layout to encourage the media to cover your project. A typical Press Kit may have any of the following items:

1. Mission Statement (*purpose of your project; who will benefit, who will do the work*)
2. Biography or Resume (*provide information about your education, athletics, clubs, volunteer work, jobs, awards, scholarships, publications, other projects, interests*)
3. List of Sponsors (*validates your project*)
4. Photo Sheet (*display photos of your project, demonstrations, speeches, community service*)
5. Publications (*select articles written by or about you, essays or research papers related to your project, or press releases*)
6. CD with photos (*jpgs ready for them to use*)

The Press Kits can be, but don't have to be, as elaborate as your Sponsor Kits. On the cover, place your project name, logo, slogan, message to the press, and the title: Press Kit. Print this out on full-sheet label paper and lay it out on each cover.

Since you will probably be dealing with the media on a regular basis, you should compile a list of all the media outlets. At a minimum, this should include local papers (small community papers love to run stories that chronicle what students are doing), but it could also include radio stations and TV stations, along with magazines and trade publications that deal with the topic of your project. Most of these media sources post their contact info online, but you should still call them to find out who the proper person is to address your correspondences to. Once you have compiled this list, you can reuse it throughout the course of your project, whenever you wish to contact the press.

Whether you're celebrating completion of a project or a milestone in a long-term project, your project deserves the attention of the press. Even if you're modest, you need to bring attention to your project. The goal is to get as much press as possible. Why? You can add each newspaper or magazine article and TV interview to your portfolio, and you can mention the press received in your personal statements and on your college application forms.

Send or drop off your News Advisory and Press Kit about a week before your event or debut. It's best to drop it off in person because it's a chance to establish rapport with the news staff. Call each contact person about 1-2 days after they receive your News Advisory and Press Kit to ensure that they did receive it and to inquire about if and when they will cover it. Remember to add this task in your planner. Don't be discouraged if reporters give noncommittal answers. Usually an editor decides what stories they will cover, and the final decision isn't made until the morning meeting the day of the event. It helps to be persistent and call the reporter the day before the event, to give them a second invitation.

If your project is a one-day event, not an on-going service, start sending your News Advisory and Press Kits to the media several months before the big day. You should also send information to be included in their Calendar Sections in the Entertainment sections of their papers if appropriate for your project. You can also build some hype around your event by getting the press to announce the event or interview you and publish your story before the event. Call the press one week, the day before, and on the morning of your event to remind them to cover your story. If your event is big enough or if there are no news-breaking events taking place that day, you may receive the press's attention.

Apply for Non-Profit Status to
Accept Donations for the Project

Many grant foundations and philanthropists will not grant money or make donations to individual people or to organizations that aren't non-profits. If your project will need substantial funding from grants, apply for non-profit status as soon as possible. Having a Federal Income Tax Exemption (501.C.3) will allow you to apply for a wide variety of grants.

Go online to **www.irs.gov/pub/irs-pdf/f1023.pdf** to print the 501.C.3 instructions and application form. Don't be alarmed by its length; only a small portion of the application will apply to you or your organization. To qualify, you'll need to set up a board of directors. Consider your mentor, teachers, and individuals involved in the industry. You'll need to get their addresses and phone numbers. By law, the members of the board of directors are not allowed to receive compensation for their participation.

The non-profit application will also request your Articles of Association and/or by-laws, which describes how your board is organized and how it functions. The easiest and quickest way to write this is to go online to review other nonprofit's bylaws or request one from a local non-profit. These by-laws are public records so organizations should readily give copies.

You'll need to apply for a Federal Tax ID number. Check online at **www.irs.gov/businesses/small/article/0**. The IRS issues these tax ID numbers for free.

Make sure you read the fine print and answer all of the required questions. If you have questions about how to fill in the application form, call (800) 829-4933. Check the instructions and submit everything they request. Make copies for your files. Mark your planner to call the IRS in one month to ensure that they received your application and to ask when you can expect notification. The IRS guarantees a response within 120 days so file early.

Apply for Grants to Finance the Project

Now that you've established your project and created the materials to promote it, you're ready to apply for grants. There are many types of grants available, but you have to track them down, narrow down the possibilities, and find the right ones to apply for. To start, inquire about possible grants from your mentor and contacts you've made in the industry. They may have applied for and received grants themselves or know about others who have. At the least, they'll know which foundations provide grants for your subject matter. Next, go online and do a search for grants, scholarships, or donations.

After completing your research to get a list of grants, request information or go online to print out grant packages. Read through them carefully to determine whether you qualify for each grant. You don't want to waste your time applying for a grant whose qualifications you cannot meet. Highlight important dates and qualifications. Read the information about past recipients to see what the committee is looking for and how it compares with your project. Call the organization to inquire about your project's potential and to get answers to your questions.

Once you establish to which foundation you will apply, enter deadlines in your planner and make a detailed list of tasks you need to complete for each grant. Then, enter each task in your planner so that the tasks will be included in your weekly schedule, and not something you do in a panic just days before the deadline. Your list of tasks may look something like this:

1. *Read through grant information for clarity and deadlines*
2. *Review your budget worksheet and add figures to meet the grant requirements*
3. *Create Board of Directors or other advisory boards required*
4. *Write bylaws or Articles of Association, if needed*
5. *Using your planner, set up timeline for project deadlines as required by organization*
6. *Identify performance standards, milestones, timelines, and tasks*
7. *Set up travel expense budget*
8. *Organize specific requirements for your grant*
9. *Make necessary copies of and label grant application*
10. *Mark and label original grant application*
11. *Review grant information sheet to ensure that you've completed all sections and packaged grant as required*
12. *Send the completed package.*

Before sending it off, double check grant requirements to make sure that you've answered their exact questions. Don't side-step questions; your application will be rejected if you don't carefully answer each of their questions. Make sure the foundation will consider individuals, organizations (check if they require non-profit status), minors, or students. When making required copies for the organization, make sure that you provide the exact number of copies and mark the original. Applications have been rejected for not having the correct number of copies and for not including the original.

Candace spent over 40 hours preparing her first grant and mailed it on the deadline. The grant foundation returned it to her unread because she forgot to include an original copy of the application form. Had she submitted the application earlier, Candace may have had the opportunity to send in the original forms and still made the deadline.

Apply for grants as soon as possible because many grants take a year or longer before funds are distributed. Most grants will not reimburse you for expenses already incurred, so don't borrow money to start the project if you expect to be reimbursed with grant funds.

Create Informational Literature: Fliers, Brochures, Logos, Business Cards to Give to Interested Parties, Sponsors, and Press

By creating informational fliers or brochures to distribute to the public, you'll establish more credibility and respect from the recipients. It is easier to understand a concept when it is laid out on a flier or brochure, than from word of mouth. Reading about the project and learning more about you add substance to your mission. By looking at photos, the reader gains a better understanding of the scope of your project.

Naturally, it's best to put together informational flier as soon as possible. Start with writing about your mission or goals, and include your bio. Just make enough copies to distribute on a weekly or case-by-case basis because this brochure will evolve with the project. You'll want to add more details and photos as you develop your project. Later, include the steps you've taken to reach your goal and photos of public outreach, research, and development. Add your flier or brochure to your Sponsor Kits and Press Kits.

If you've never designed a flier or brochure, start by looking at other brochures. Check your school counseling office, doctor's offices, and Chamber of Commerce or Visitor's Center. You can also request brochures from industry organizations. By looking at other fliers and brochures, you can determine which styles, colors, and paper you prefer. You can use a brochure template from word-processing programs or you can purchase one online. The easiest and least expensive brochure to print is the 8 1/2" x 11", double-sided, 3-panel brochure. It fits easily into a standard #10 business envelope and requires only regular postage.

Sketch your brochure layout to determine where text, photos, and logos will be placed. This helps you determine how much information you can include before you begin writing. By designing a tri-fold brochure, you'll save money because you won't need odd-sized envelopes since #10 business standard envelopes are inexpensive. With the tri-fold brochure, you'll have 6 panels to fill with information about your project. Each panel can address different aspects of your project. For example, Panel 1 can introduce your project with your logo, slogan, and contact info, Panel 2 can lay out your mission statement and goals, Panel 3 can state how to volunteer, Panel 4 can invite people to sign up for your services, Panel 5 can have your bio and photo, and Panel 6 can list your sponsors and testimonials (endorsements). Consider the margins created by folds. Set your titles and subtitles using the same size font and attributes. Include photos, clipart, or graphs to grab the readers' attention.

For fliers, the layout is less complicated than brochures because they are single sided and generally have less information. Decide whether you want to use letter (8 ½" x 11") or legal (8 ½" x 14") size paper. Then place your logo, slogan, and contact information. Next, create sections for the same information listed in the brochure above. You can use columns or created borders around each section. Use a larger font and condense the text. People usually don't spend a lot of time reading the fine print on fliers as they might for a brochure. State important information and provide pull-off tabs at the bottom of the flier that they can take with them. Include your logo, phone, and a few words to describe your project to remind them of the reason they grabbed the tab.

Business cards are nice to have because you can carry them with you in your wallet. By placing your logo, business name, slogan, and contact information (name, title, address, phone, grade level or age, email address, and website), this business card contains all pertinent information in a small

space. Examine other business cards to determine your preference on layout. You can lay out your card landscape (the longest side is horizontal) or portrait (the longest side is vertical). Some business cards have color photos. Hand them out to prospective sponsors, volunteers, clients/customers, or the press.

If you're familiar with desktop-publishing programs such as InDesign or Quark, you can produce a professional-looking product. Other programs, such as Word, also allow you the ability to add photos and graphs and to set up columns, and they also have brochure templates. If designing your own logo or laying out your brochure is too much to do yourself, stores like Kinkos have services that design and print brochures, fliers, and business cards.

All of your printed media can be printed on your home printer or at your local copy center. Some copy centers may reduce the price of their services once you tell them about your project, especially if they know you are a nonprofit. Inquire about this. You may need to write a letter requesting a donation. Include your Sponsor Kit and offer to add them as an official sponsor of your project.

Set up a Website to Promote Your Project on the Internet

The internet has become the 21st century's answer to the bulletin board. By creating a website for your project, you'll be able to post your information for the entire world to see. With user-friendly site building software such as WordPress, you can easily create your own website. Enlist the help or guidance of friends or family members who have built websites.

You'll need to purchase a domain name (the name used before the dot com) and purchase space from a hosting provider to store your site and serve it to visitors. Your domain name is very important, as it's the main way people will access your site. Try to use some form of the title of your organization, business, or project name. If your preferred domain name is already taken, try rewording using a different extension like .org. After you've selected a domain name, choose a hosting provider. Most hosting providers will also allow you to purchase your domain name from them, often at a discount. Check around to see what services and restrictions each host provides. Some limit the size of your website. Some offer live support for free while others charge. Check to see if the hosting company offers free email addresses so you can have an email address that matches your website domain. If your project is a non-profit or a community service, try requesting that the hosting company become a sponsor by donating the space.

To get started, lay out a website flowchart that outlines how your pages are interconnected and how you expect the users to navigate your site. First decide how you want the site to look. If you're not familiar with HTML or have never designed a website before, you may want to use a template so your website will look professional. Place your logo, organization name, and slogan at the top of the page. Choose the color scheme if that's an option with your template. Be sure to limit the number of words you use for the page titles, as long titles will make your top navigation too wide and difficult to read. Each web page can represent each section of your brochure.

For instance, your pages may include Mission Statement, Project History, Photo History, Volunteers, About, Contact Us, and Home.

There are some basic web design techniques to consider when laying out your page. Some of the biggest design problems are as follows: the color scheme is too loud, making the user distracted or the text too hard to read; fonts are too big, making the text hard to read because it stretches across the screen (columns are much easier to read); too many links or too much text may be overwhelming, especially on the initial pages (simple sites are more effective; the really elaborate details should be beneath more general and easy-to-read information); navigation is convoluted, making it difficult to find basic information. When in doubt, browse the internet for ideas and choose colors and styles that appeal to you.

Write the text for your website in a word-processing program that has spell checking and make sure to proofread. You will be able to take text from other places like your Press Kits, Press Releases, News Advisories, fliers and brochures. Once the text is the way you want it, enter the same text on the appropriate pages on your site.

Don't forget social media! You'll want to create social media accounts for your project on all the popular services as a way to get your message out. Make sure you link to each of those services from your website. The website is the hub - if someone sees a post you make on social media, they'll go to your site to get more information.

After your website is live, you'll need to test it and get feedback from friends and your mentor. Don't be disappointed if links don't work or if photos won't open when you first put up your website. Ask friends, or others who are not familiar with your project, to explore your website. Use their feedback to make necessary improvements so that your site is user-friendly. You'll want your visitors to your website to be able to easily move from page to page and to reach their destination within just a few clicks. Most visitors won't spend more than a few seconds trying to find the information they are looking for before they give up.

Websites also need to appeal to the visual senses. Even if the text is interesting, your site will seem boring without pictures and graphics. Select photos of you working at various stages on your project. Include photos of you doing research, meeting with your mentor and working on the project. Using captions below each photo, describe what it is you are doing. In order for the browser to open your pages quickly, photos for your website should not be gigantic, and pages shouldn't have dozens of pictures.

Organize Your Event

If your project culminates with a presentation or an event, you'll need to carefully plan out all of details to ensure that your big day runs smoothly. After all, you've worked hard conducting the research, designing your organization's logos and marketing plan, and preparing Press Kits for your debut. Sharpen your pencil and begin by creating a timeline for the day of the event. Spend a few minutes thinking about how your event will run. From the start of your event, consider when and where each facet will take place. This mental review of your event timeline will help you understand the structure so that you can organize the many details. When you have this mental picture of the structure of your event, you'll be ready to begin to organize it. You can write directly in your planner (on the event's date), or you can start by writing on a pad of paper and then transfer the timeline into your planner later. Consider the following tasks and questions when organizing your event.

1. *When will the facility be available to me for my event?*
2. *Who are the contact people/managers for the facility? Get their phone numbers (cell phone numbers would be ideal) so you can reach them in an emergency.*
3. *Can you set up the night before? Can you store materials at the site ahead of time?*
4. *Will you need electricity? Where are the outlets? Will you need extension cords? What lengths of extension cords will you need? Does the facility require that you use gaffer's tape to secure all electrical cords? Check with the manager to make sure that your electrical cords will meet the fire marshal's requirements for fire safety.*
5. *Will you need lighting? Most facilities offer basic lighting for free, but charge if you use special spot lights or specialized lighting fixtures. Will you handle the lighting, or will you need a designated person to be responsible for your lighting?*
6. *Will you need a sound system (Microphones, microphone stands, mixer, amplifier, receiver, speakers, speaker stands, monitor)? If the facility*

doesn't supply the items you need, will you rent them? When can you pick up the items, and when do they need to be returned? Who will pick them up and in what vehicle? Will you need to supply fresh batteries? When will you buy them? Always have extras, just in case you need them.

7. Will you need audio visual aids (overhead projector, laptop, PowerPoint)?

8. Will you need a kitchen facility? Check out the site to ensure that you'll have enough refrigerator or freezer space, cooking equipment, and serving dishes and utensils. Do you need a permit from the Department of Environmental Health?

9. Will you need a lectern, podium, stage, tables, or chairs? Does the facility already have this equipment or do you have to rent them? If you need to rent them, when can you pick up the items? When will the items need to be returned? Who will help you transport them to and from the facility? What vehicle will you use?

10. What decorations do you plan to use? Will you need tablecloths to cover tables? Where will you get them and who will be responsible for making sure they're clean and pressed? Will you have balloons, plants, banners, or posters? What items do you need and how will you display them? Where will you get them?

11. What other things do you need to present your project or to run your event? List things to buy, to rent, and to borrow here.

12. How many people will you need to help you set up for the event? Will you need these people for the entire event or just for set up and break down? What time do you want them to arrive and where will they meet you? Do you have their cell phone numbers and other contact information?

13. Are there enough restroom facilities for your guests? If not, you'll need to rent a port-o-potty. What time would you like these delivered? When will they be picked up?

14. Will you have photographers or videographers there to capture your event in the form of photos or videotapes? Will you be supplying the cameras, film, tapes, and batteries? When will you buy the supplies and charge the batteries? Make a list of what scenes or parts of the event you would like your photographer and videographer to get.

15. Will you need the police to handle traffic? You'll need to contact the city police department to request police support, if necessary. Will you use balloons to help guests find your event? Who will blow them up or purchase them? Who will set them up?

16. Will there be enough parking spaces available to handle all of your guests? If not, will you direct guests to park elsewhere? Will you need to set up a shuttle to transport guests to your event?

17. Will you need to clean the facility at the end of your event? If you do, how many helpers will you need and how much time will it take to clean up.

18. *Who do you meet with at the end of the event to return keys, sign contract, receive deposit back, or pay fees? Get this person's contact information to ensure that you won't be waiting for them when you're all set to leave.*

After you've compiled your list, delegate tasks to your volunteers (or family and friends). Keep accurate records so you can remind each volunteer what their responsibilities are. It's best to make a list for each volunteer (keep a copy for yourself) so they can make plans around your event. Then, place all of your tasks (the ones you didn't delegate to others) in your planner. Next, place your volunteers' tasks in your planner using a different color ink or off in the margins so you'll know what others will be doing. One week before the event, email your volunteers to remind them of the tasks and times for their participation. Sometimes volunteers forget about commitments and make other plans. If you have any irresponsible people in your group, you'll want to learn about that in time so you can recruit someone to replace them. You'll also want to stay in touch with all of the volunteers during the week before the event, and on the night before, call everyone to review their responsibilities and to make sure that they're ready. By giving volunteers a written description of their tasks and exact dates and times to perform them in addition to phoning them and talking to them, you're setting yourself up for the best odds that everyone will fulfill their part. You'll be able to use these leadership skills in all facets of your life.

After you make sure that your volunteers are organized, it's time to organize yourself. Review your list and enter in your planner more details about what and when you need to do each task. If you need to purchase things, block off time to buy the items way in advance so you won't be running errands on the morning of your event. Start collecting your items ahead of time, like weeks ahead, and put them in a box or safe place. Make banners, signs, and posters and store them in tubes to protect them. If you're doing a demonstration, make sure that everything is in working order. Set up a backup solution in case something goes wrong. If you're doing a presentation, practice your speech so you're comfortable with it. Block off time to deliver your speech to your parents or friends. Review the entire timeline to make sure you haven't forgotten something important. When you spend time thinking, and rethinking, the process through, your event will run smoothly.

Brent, a drummer, organized a music festival for kids. He chose this project to introduce young children to the world of music. He decided to have his music festival in a local park, where he set up three stages. Each stage sectioned off different instruments for children to watch and to try: (1) Guitars; (2) Keyboards; and (3) Drums. Brent sent out fliers to all of the music schools, private music teachers, and school band teachers to encourage students to play at his festival. Brent designed and built the platforms for his three stages with his friends so they would be easy to assemble at the park. He brought in his own sound system for one stage, borrowed one from his band teacher for the second, and rented additional microphones and speakers from a local rental company for the third. He borrowed his uncle's truck and rallied Alex and Nick, 2 members from his band, to help him transport the stage and equipment to the park at 8:00 am on the day of the event. Alex was assigned the task of setting up the sound system for all three stages, while Nick assembled the stages. Nicole, a girl who takes guitar lessons from one of the music schools, blew up the balloons and placed them according to the map that Brent drew for her on the traffic signals with directional signs. Brent placed all of his posters, banners, and signs and set up his information booth for guests and the press. He laid out his Press Kits and fliers for guests, and he set up a donation can. As the teen musicians arrived, he showed them where to set up their equipment and discussed their performance schedule. Brent invited the press to meet him 3 hours before the event started. He gave them his Press Kits and answered questions in the interviews. His volunteers seated the families on the grass as they arrived. Armed with a wireless microphone, Brent introduced the musicians on all of the stages and invited children to try playing the instruments after each performance. At the end of the event, Brent and his volunteers picked up the trash and loaded the truck with the equipment. His event was covered in the local paper and he put the article and photo in his portfolio. Brent's music festival was a huge success, largely due to his organizational skills.

Invite Press to See Completion of Your Project – The Interview

Congratulations! You've completed your project and now you're ready to tell the world. Some projects (festivals, inventions) will culminate with an event or debut, while others (educational outreach, program development) may be an ongoing process. The media is always interested in grand openings or the release of important research. Many newspapers will cover stories on teens doing special projects, especially unique or community service projects. When this happens, it is important to convey a positive image and to get your message across with enthusiasm and accuracy. Talking to a reporter is different than talking to most people, so it is important to be careful. Remember that reporters are neither your friend nor your enemy; they simply want to hear what you have to say and report it.

You don't have to obsess over every word you say, but you cannot be careless either. Before meeting with reporters, it is wise to first think about what you plan to tell them (and what you don't want to tell them). Reporters are busy people, so they don't have the time to talk about every detail of your project. You only need to give them a general overview. Make sure you know your facts and jot down information you want to cover. This is easier than trying to remember when you're on the spot. Make sure that you only say things that you know are accurate and that portray you positively. Anything you say is fair game for them to report. Think about how it would look if it got back to thousands of people.

Wear appropriate clothing, especially if you are going to be photographed or filmed. You don't need to buy a $500 suit, but don't wear a dirty t-shirt and old jeans either, nor should you wear flashy or indecent clothing. You may want to wear an outfit that relates to your project, since this would make a good photo. If you're building something, wear work clothes and be prepared to demonstrate your project.

Always introduce yourself with a handshake and make good eye contact. Invite the interviewer into a quiet place in your home or classroom so you won't be interrupted or distracted during the interview. Be enthusiastic about your project. If this is a TV interview or if a newspaper photographer is present, act natural and smile for the cameras.

Afterwards, collect copies of all media about your project to include in your portfolio. For radio and TV shows, you may have to purchase tapes for a nominal fee. Ask someone at the station how this works. For print media, find out when the article is going to run (though dates often change) and clip it out.

Update Website with Completion of Your Project

After you have completed your project and met with the press, it's time to update your website. Add photos of your event and quotes or testimonials from participants. If you received press, add a video clip of TV coverage, audio clip of radio interviews, and scanned copies of printed press. You'll need to acknowledge the photographer. Simply state "Photographs courtesy of _____".

Updating your website will announce to the public that you completed your project as planned. Your mentor and teachers who will write your letters of recommendation can visit your website to learn more about your project, which will encourage them to write strong letters of recommendation. College admissions officers may view your website to verify that you did indeed complete the project and build the website as stated in your personal statements.

Set up Project to Continue Without You
When You Go to College

If your project is a community service, train other students and volunteers who can run the program after you leave. You may need to set up a Board of Directors, if you didn't already do that for your non-profit status. By working with the Board, you set up the program to continue in your absence. You can also stay involved via email or phone conferences.

"Many projects set up by college-bound students don't end with high school or college admissions. The ultimate test may be determined by whether or not your project can continue without you."

If appropriate, you can start a sister organization or an extension of the same organization at your new college. Since the project is already up and running and you already have lots of experience, this will be considerably less work and less time consuming to start. Add your new location on your website and solicit volunteers among your college peers. College students tend to be motivated and can devote more time and energy to extracurricular endeavors.

At college, you may have access to more funding sources, many of which will fund you without requiring an extensive application process. Look to students clubs, student government, and the student union to see if they offer funding. Often, these organizations have hundreds of dollars to spend, and will distribute it to groups that are aligned with their goals. They may ask you to give a public presentation about your goals.

The College Application Essay

If you've completed your project by the summer after your junior year, you're ready to start the college application process. Assuming you've already selected the colleges to which you'd like to apply, go online to review the application and instructions. Many colleges require a personal statement and several short essays or responses. The prompts tend to give you some leeway with what to focus on.

The goal is to talk about your project when you write these essays, but this is easier said than done, because you will need to be able to relate the project to their prompt or essay topic in way that is convincing. Read through the personal statement topics carefully to determine how you can discuss your project while still addressing their prompt.

To help you get started, first brainstorm about why you started the project, and then how you organized it. Discuss what you learned and how you felt. Then, write an outline to help you set up the framework for your essay. Your outline might look something like this:

1. *Chose project. (Why did you choose this project? Describe your passions or concerns)*
2. *Found mentor and role mentor played*
3. *Set up non-profit status for sponsorships and funding*

4. Applied for grants and scholarships (Discuss what funding you received)
5. Designed brochure, flier, website (Discuss where you distributed the information)
6. Implemented project (Discuss obstacles you encountered and how you overcame them)
7. Current state of project (Describe your expectations, what you learned, how it impacted others, your plans for the future)

Your tone should be both enthusiastic and modest. Tell them about exciting moments when milestones were met as well as lessons learned from mistakes made. They'll appreciate your candor and see that you've learned good life skills and that you're a leader who doesn't quit. Remember that admissions counselors are looking for specific attributes in their applicants: leadership potential, ability to overcome obstacles, special talents, creativity. By discussing your project, you can illustrate these qualities.

Be sure to include start and end dates to emphasize that your project wasn't simply a teacher's assignment that was completed in a semester or a passing fancy that occupied you for only a few weeks. This will show that you have the ability to construct a long-term vision, plan and research how to achieve it, and lead it to fruition.

The college admissions officers will be interested in your leadership role in how the project was implemented and how your project will affect the community or the greater world.

Remember that colleges hope to admit a class full of students who will graduate from their institutions and go on to become successful professionals and leaders. By effectively writing your essay to show them that you have already demonstrated in high school what they hope you might do when you graduate from college will give you the edge on admissions. There's no doubt that when given two students with similar application packages (identical GPA's and SAT scores) the student who has completed a project will be admitted before the one who hasn't.

Beyond College Admissions

Although you may be doing the project to help ensure acceptance into selective universities, you'll gain much more than just that. As you take the necessary steps to complete the project, you'll be learning life and professional skills that will make you successful for the rest of your life.

The brainstorming you did to select your project is similar to the brainstorming you may do to select a project to get you into the graduate school of your choice. Like undergraduate admissions, selective graduate schools admit students who have shown a passion in their discipline and that they have already started a project before entering their institution.

By learning how to organize a project, you'll be able to write a business or marketing plan and plan events. Your time management skills will help you squeeze more tasks into a 24-hour day. Using your planner, you could layout the entire project to ensure that each step is met by its deadline.

If you receivd grant money or sponsorships, you'll already be seasoned to write grants for future research, business, or projects. Most adults don't have the knowledge or skills to apply for grants. You'll also have a portfolio already filled with moneys received for other projects – something other students probably won't have when competing for the same grants.

Whether you're applying to graduate schools, starting a business, or beginning a professional career, you'll want the press to acknowledge you. You'll know how to put together impressive Press and Sponsor Kits to get those interviews with local newspaper, radio stations, and TV stations. Educating the public about what you are doing will certainly boost your business and clientele. When applying for a job, you'll know how to put together an impressive resume.

What you'll learn about working with volunteers, government agencies, private businesses, professionals, and others is an invaluable life skill. Simply by implementing your project, you'll inevitably run into delays with poorly-run organizations, deadlines not met by people with good intentions, inaccurate information printed by the press, and

other obstacles. Learning these lessons in high school will better prepare you to avoid these problems in college and career.

Even after you graduate from college and have started your career, the skills you learned by starting your project can help you advance your career. You'll know how to work with the press to announce new developments and you'll know how to implement changes. If you're looking for a corporate promotion, you'll know how to layout out your accomplishments in a professional format to impress your supervisors. Or if you're looking for a career change or a company change, you'll know how to brainstorm and set up a plan to implement your change.

And finally, someday you'll probably be a spouse and parent. Juggling career and family takes planning, organization, and team work. You'll have a better handle on time management and planning than others simply because by using your planner, you'll know how to block off time to complete tasks and how to manage all aspects of your life. These leadership skills are invaluable in all aspects of your personal and professional life.

Final Words of Advice: Do This Project Yourself (but not all by yourself)

This project is your project, and your project alone. That means that you are in charge and you are responsible for every aspect of the project. Your mentor and parents can offer guidance, suggestions, and even some collaboration—but they should not run the project or do your work.

At every science fair, there's at least one student whose parents obviously did the work for their child. Remember how everyone else looked down upon that person? You don't want that person to be you. You'll want to be able to say, with honesty, that you started and completed the project on your own. If your parents made phone calls, put together Press or Sponsor Kits, conducted your experiment, or managed your project, others will think that your parents did the project for you. Part of the project is building your personal integrity.

Bob and Judy, retired scientists, wanted their only son Cameron to be accepted to one of their alma maters. Rather than allowing Cameron to do his project, they actually did his project for him. They set up his mentors, requested materials for his grants, wrote his budget and put together his grants, and assisted him at his demonstrations and presentations, and even wrote his college application essays. While Cameron did get admitted to Judy's alma mater, he wasn't prepared for the rigorous work. After a semester, Cameron dropped out and was back at home attending the local community college. Not only did he mislead the admissions committee, but he also set himself up for failure.

You want to earn the right of admission to the college of your choice because of your hard work. If you do the project on your own, you're preparing yourself to succeed in college and beyond. If your parents do your project, you'll probably have difficulty succeeding in college on your own (you can't take them with you to college!). So start now by doing this project by yourself.

Some students are tempted to partner up with a friend and run the project together. This is also a bad idea. Not only will you lose the bragging rights, but this can actually trip you up. What would happen if your partner loses interest halfway through? What if they get other ideas about what you should be doing?

What if you cannot agree about a major decision? What if your schedules become incompatible? Just like in business, it's not recommended to work with friends or family, because it compromises your personal relationship. If you feel like the project is so big that it needs two people in charge, it's wiser to narrow down your focus to something more managea

Best friends since 6th grade, Ryan and Darin decided to collect soccer equipment from players at the end of the season to give to underprivileged kids in Mexico. Ryan, the outgoing personality, agreed to create the flyers and contact all of the coaches in the county to pass along the message about their project. Darin, the more demure personality, agreed to write the News Advisory and put together the Press Kits. Unbeknownst to Ryan, Darin was unsure of what to do and too embarrassed to ask for help. He hadn't contacted the press or put together his end of the partnership. Meanwhile, Ryan had sent emails

> "Remember that this project will not only help you get into your top-choice colleges, but it will help you learn life-long skills that you might not learn in college or career."

to the coaches and posted fliers at every game for a two month period at the end of the school year. When Ryan learned that Darin didn't put together anything for the press, Ryan verbally attacked Darin and stormed off to get the job done himself. With the late notice to the press, they missed a great opportunity to expand their coverage and results, and to get their story covered in the paper. Not only did this ruin their friendship, but Ryan had to share the success of the project with a partner who didn't contribute.

CONCLUSION

Now get going. Start by going back to the beginning of this book and taking it one step at a time. You'll need to use your planner to help manage your busy schedule to ensure that you can continue to get good grades, prepare for the SATs, and do the project. Remember that this project will not only help you get into your top-choice colleges, but it will help you learn life-long skills that you might not learn in college or career. So, you're investing in your future, today. Congratulations on taking the first step.

SUPPORT

Susan Tatsui-D'Arcy, author and college advisor, works with college-bound students nationwide. If you need guidance and support, call her at (831) 462-5655 or check out her online support at **www.meritworld.com**.